up down, down up

A.R. Adamyk

contents

down *4*

up...*98*

*to help you feel
not so alone
in this great big
world*

down

a happy ending
where do i find you
pain
it's pulling me down
the deeper i go
the surface
unseen
moving down
there is no end
sinking deeper
i want to break up
above
to that surface
but how can i
the deeper i go
the harder it is to rise
support for me
has dwindled
the dark parts
are dragging me
down
away from up
above

there's a war
a great one
fighting within
i can't distinguish
after all
i let it in

i'm always
so blue
the darkest shade
never true
to who i am
hidden
in the deepest
unseen places
closing in
away
from focus

i'm just
someone
who
people
tolerate
all the things
i am
do
you
all
tolerate
it

most people come
into this world
alone
when you're alone
no one can disappoint you

discarded
unwanted
depressed
under the blankets
unwilling to leave
unwilling to live

it's all karma
the way i'm born
i deserve it

sometimes
i want to say goodbye
then i remember
all the love
that's in the air
that isn't fair
the love would linger
forever in pain
if i ever did say goodbye
so why would i want to die
sometimes that's cruel

that boy
in the past
he was a failure
no wonder
no one liked him
i don't either
even now

am i happy
one day maybe
i hope i find happiness
i've forgotten its look

racism
derogatory haze
homophobia
beds deep
within man
the male gaze
the powerful
masculinity
within the bully
i've battled
from it
i have forever
embedded in me
a lasting
disdain
towards
men

i am loved
yet i don't see this love
where is it
how can i feel it
i don't wake up with it
i don't go to sleep with it
you say you love me
but where
i wanna see it
but how can i
when i am so far gone
i barely show up for it

a 7-year-old takes pills
to calm them
to down their personality
when they're already
unaccepted
hidden
you take them
in hopes to be normal
to not be anyone else
yet they try
to simply just be
this type of way
because that's all they are
so far

kids do grow
hating who they are
because there is disdain
built around them
on their nature
their fear when growing
continues
into adulthood
to hate them
and others

that hurting
possessive feeling
of wanting him
it poisons my mind
continuously
i know he'll never
feel the torture
of this love game
he'll never wonder
the pain
he's put me
under

new to town
a shiny toy
looking for friends
used up so fast
put aside
once your climax ends

you promised a bike ride
a love
a day together
a promise once served
now ignored
left to cry
so why pry
for someone
who will just lie

it wasn't the getting over you
that was hard
it was the getting to myself
that was hard
…it's still hard

download
share
scare
love
leave
empty

the touch we wanted
passed us so fast
once you finished
i was left
done with
just for your amusement
for fun in the long run
never lasted in my favour

how foolish
i came to you
we touched
pleasure was given
just like that
then asked to leave
i was empty

i remember still
all your faces
the bullies
in all my private places
your shades
follow me
even into these later days
the scars you sprayed
stay

i've been shot
arrows coming at me
from child
to adult
it gets worse
i've shot arrows
to you
to them
due to all the fires
striking me
all the hurt
i've been dealt
i've shot right back
i'd like to say
i'm sorry

wanting to die
sometimes
is better than
always
wanting to

better today
scared for tomorrow
i may not be okay
i'm sick of feeling this way
how do i ever make it to tomorrow
and all the days that follow
somehow
i do
i hate it

you give me something
i'll give you something
we'll walk away
empty handed
forget each other
forget the pleasure
but thank you
because we both found
a little treasure

you presented yourself
in my bubble
inserted yourself into me
used me
i let you
it was the right thing
for us both to do
how wrong was i
to be treated in such a lie
you lay there
unfazed
by the hurting
in the air
i hid it away
like i didn't care
but i so did
did you

i hurt easy
it's from all the growing
it was never easy
all the voices
judges
watching me fall
to the ground
never getting up
only to cry
consumed
by all the hurt
it takes over who i am
life now
holds on
to all the judges
all the easy hurting
it's just who i am
hurting

i wanted to connect
instead i stayed in bed
i hoped you'd come
knocking on my door
inviting me
to see the colours
the kisses
the clothes
the queerness of it all
but instead
my anxiety made me fall
deep into that safe bed
i so desperately wanted
all that was you
and then some
yet i stayed away
i have been for so long
when will it end
i wanna live now
because my younger self
he didn't

those words
at age 11
in the halls
i wanted to die
the words at 15
i still wanted to die
after it came to an end
i left
still wanting to die
even today
the triggers come forth
they make me feel ill
yet now i don't want to die
only sometimes
that's better
than all those times

as i came of age
i knew i was different
in the eyes of my friends
most importantly my family
my voice didn't deepen
my body
ashamed
i became so desperate
to be liked
to be like everyone
but everyone
they hurt me
i was so different
why did i become so hated
why did i exist
i wondered
people with difference
where's their acceptance
where was mine
why do i exist

it's a joke really
this life thing
leading me on
as i keep growing
i wonder
to earlier days
why didn't i end
i guess i'm wrong
in ending
i've just got to keep going
you do to
so we can find
an unending

i fear to lose
i fear to love
i fear to change
after all i've been dealt
i am triggered
just by wanting
to simply live
this is all i've felt
i shall keep it that way
shouldn't i
but that's not fair
no
we mustn't

growing up
untaught
uncultured
unsupported
left to be tortured
yelled at
inside and outside
that's just what it's like
growing up
the diverse one
the different one
that's our grow up

in the name of the father
the son
the holy spirit
the men
the words
the pain
the torture
the killing
the suffering
in the name of their power
let it sour
devour them whole
for they take and take
i dare you
try again
for we stand tall
over the mighty who made us fall

rejection is a part of me
a part of you
the one who started it
i'm still here
moving forward
yet somehow still dealing
are you?
the one less appealing
for me
the rejection
is always there
i try not to see it
most days it's visible
because of you
the bully

i see the ones i love
falling in love
i know i can never have
the boys
i secretly adore
it hurts me
weakens me to my core
forever knowing
a love i want
will never form
in a place
only grown
for abuse

once again
i lay with a man
he does so with me
i feel rotten
does he
come the next day
we will have both forgotten

late night drive
places of uncertainty
unknown
that's the thrill of it all
the heart races
the first looks
the touches
the kisses
it's blissful for the short time
but when the night is over
you leave empty
maybe used
in pain
more alone
then ever before
that's the way we are
when will it stop
how do we end this pain
we so desperately cling to
i guess in time
we'll see
for now
we'll be numb

the guilt
after the bed
the kissing
the sex
is it right
to be so confessing
with someone
so unwilling

some days i can't hold back
i just want the day over

am i anything
or am i obsolete
how come i do and do
but receive no welcome
i feel so behind
not so refined
at anything at all
what shall i do

i want the sweat on the skin
the cream
the wetness of men
is it so much to ask
this anxiety stops me
from all that i want and am

you looked at me
said i was pretty
thank you came out of me
then i noticed
the pushing
of your body
when i did
i saw uncertainty
did i want it
no

some days
i love myself
my body
who i am
then other days
i think i want to die
these thoughts
are just aimless
pieces of paper
forgotten notes
i discard them
but then
i make new ones
when will it end

i've hurt you
you didn't deserve it
i apologize sincerely
i know what it's like
so please be alright
i am deeply sorry
for the fight

you took me
loved me
kissed me
touched me
fucked me
used me
left me
foolishly
i still want it
pain and all

multiple partners
new
exciting
the first touches
wetness
nervous hands
sweaty messes
yet it ends so quick
will it ever be real

i cry for the attention
i can't stop
for when something eats you from inside
you can't scream the suffering
because it hurts
so when i cry
i hope
they see the truth
hiding inside
under the tears

where do i go
when i can't see

i've rehearsed being alone
repeatedly
to see what i want
to be where i want
alone
without a lover
to hold me back
i can do it alone
i don't need you
you don't need me
it's bleak and disheartening
we grow as individuals
alone

i'm incapable to die
but god knows
i consider it

i know
it doesn't make sense
i hate me
i love me
opposites attract
how can i live
loving and hating
who i am

it's just one day
or more
of bumpy
unstable
emotions
it'll pass
i'm just so unsure

i hurt someone
that was never my intention
i thought i made a friend in them
but i misjudged
as i usually do

my life is privileged
my life has air to breathe
my life has a body to move
with all these things
i feel so wrong
how can that be
is it the dark and light
within me
stuck in my mind
i should be happy
under a roof
tucked in bed
yet i'm hurting
how do we get out of this state
why do we feel like this
we should be happy right
what is wrong with our minds
the conclusion is
nothing…
but it's hard to see it that way
the bad thoughts are strong
they take control
make us feel like nothing
but we aren't nothing
and nothing is wrong with us
it is life
and some day
we'll be okay

the pain giver
sits there
in my mind
taking control of me
yes i allowed them in
am i a victim
i guess not
because i opened the door
in hopes of good
as he left
i walked away
from me
stayed with him
the hurter
that was never my intention

just when i think i have hold
of some sort of happiness
my mind comes and breaks it
and i see memories shatter like a mirror
and i conclude
those good thoughts
they never mattered
they were always meant
to be shattered

i was fed with lies
filling my heart
even after the loving
always hungry for more
i'm still wishing
you stayed forever
sealed on me
like bad ink

well
being queer
is not something lightly
every day
my mind
goes to dark places
so unsure
that's just a packaged deal
oh dear

i didn't want to talk about it
i didn't even know it
as a kid
i had no one to relate to
to explain to
who was i
to everyone around me
they were simply
able to be
what about me

have i ever tried
there's no clear answer
do i want to die
i don't know
are others suicidal
do they want to live
unlike me who's tired
have i ever truly tried
these thoughts keep us here
thank god we them
otherwise
we'd be gone
and i don't think others want that
do we

have i ever loved me
without pretending to show others
through a screen

i'll never be the one someone wants

i want others to know
the pain
the waking up
the crowds
the anxiety
are we okay
am i okay

30 is practically here
oh dear
what have i done
was it fun
will i ever get near
to what i don't know
when does it come
will it all be clear
or will there still be fear

so misunderstood
never feeling good
why is there no answer

i get to the next day
only to shy away
hurt
cracks
scars
depression
who really listens

i'm so lonesome
without you
beside me
laughing with me
holding me
touching me
you along with them
passed so quickly
i see why now
i'm so lonesome
i wasn't ready
i'll never be
with ones like you

how do i feel whole
without all shots
coming at me
it's become regular
hole after hole
patch after patch
it's only getting worse
what can i do to feel whole

i think i'm always
a work in progress
never able
to reach
the progress
i work on myself
only to be shut down
by myself
watching others
get their progress
as i'm failing behind
by me and my mind
i've always been like this
how do i stop
when the world won't stop
all the progress
i can never be a part of

night calls
i lay alone
to touch
to be touched
how can i
when so afraid
so unable
so ashamed

i hurt easy
i cry easy
growing up wasn't easy
even now
starting the 30's
hurting is there
can't i just have it easy now
please
oh right
don't be silly…
it's not that easy

i can't help
but fall for the ones
who desert me
or the ones
who kiss me just once
and leave me in the dust
will i ever fall in love

this was physical pain
mixed with emotional pain
i was thrown onto my own bed
your touch was pleasant
but so fast
you took advantage
the arms around my throat
the pleasures i received
the cries i leaked
you pushed me to my limit
i couldn't speak
you kept pushing me
holding me
escaping wasn't an option
and it hurt
there was no communication
in my own bed
i was humiliated
as soon as we finished
you left
and i looked in the mirror
and saw flesh unknown

- sexual abuse

failing thoughts
they hit hard
i'm watching those around me
grow
flourish
be the truest
where i fail
to get up
exercise the mind
i feel behind
i'm not where i want to be
the anxiety hinders me
it has failed me
how can i move on
when my mind stalls me
i watch everyone
find the now
find the life
while i sit and cry
shiver
eat
don't eat
i wonder
through all the loathing
does anyone even love me
i loved
once upon a time
down another road
i've nothing else to say
except
i'm in pain
unimaginable
i want it to end
please
when

- depression

i'm not okay
i say it out loud
finally
hoping someone
hears me
but no one can
not even me
all the thoughts
drown me out
did i even say it

you broke me
didn't even know
don't worry
i wouldn't rat you out
even though
i shattered

i'm so lonely
stuck in my sheets
blinds closed
unable to move
eating isn't an option
i'm broken down
like a baby bird
pinned from the rain
healing won't come
only endless streams of pain
the wounds hurt
slowly
as the light strikes
from the cracks of those closed blinds
i awake
to find someone
he's still alone

those memories
in childhood times
bring up pains
unimaginable to you
in my adulthood days
i'll never let this go

i'm becoming less like me every day
and it scares me

i was once in love
with happiness
it was a love so regular
a love that lasted
now it's sour to the taste
it's become irregular

i'm devoid of self love
i don't have answers
the hate has always been there
hiding like scum under a ship
i've always been this way
i don't know how not to
that little boy
he and i
think the same

i'm drunk right now
and this is the realist it's gonna be
and the worst it's gonna be
just love me now
but if you can't handle it well
let us leave it at that
no!
fuck you for not loving me
but i wouldn't either
if i saw me
an abused wonderer

when i saw you
it happened so fast
first the innocence
then the kiss
then the violence
then the demand
you stripped me
you pushed me
you pinned me
you touched me
you sucked the confidence
out of me
you left me
feeling rotten
to my core
moving on
will never be easy
and you won't know
how it feels
until gosh forbid
it happens to you
you selfish
you handsome
you kind
you facade
you abuser

happiness is right there
it is sweet
and tasteful
how come i don't want it
who does
after all they've been through
it's become a regular taunt now

bruises on my neck
left behind
from your kisses
as i watched you leave
i looked in the mirror
saw someone else
after all that occurred
i just let it happen
what could i have done
in the moment
my voice was pushed back
by all your manhood
that place of safety
was taken from me
i'm still here
i want to be
but i'm anxious
broken
confused
though as time passed
i've taken back
my voice
and all the kisses
i now have ones to give
in consent
but i'm scared to
because of you

i want it so bad
a true love
some days i can almost taste it
where is this person
who will love
my individual self
they don't exist in my world
i don't feel it or see it
maybe because
i'm not one
with it
this self love
they all talk about

26 - depressed, hurt, fun
27 - uncertain, pain, relaxed
28 - free, up, down,
don't turn around

- anxiety, stress, pandemic, years past, trauma, abuse

the dancing
the smiles
it's all a façade
advertising the fakest parts
those days
i'm just ignoring
all that's inside
the cuts
the bruises
the abuser
to simply get by
no one knows an end
not even your closest friend
it all becomes so real
that you aren't
and that's the scary part
no one knows the real you
through this structure
not even you
don't ever go there
please i beg of you
i know this pain all too well
reach out
scream if you must
break the structure
please don't leave us
because we really do
love you

maybe i'm healing
i just don't see it
right now i'm hurting
lost
forgotten
can't get out of bed
maybe that's the journey
rest
recharge
bring a safer
newer version
to the light you hide from
once i'm done
i will see it
the healing
the parts of me
that are fresh
regrown
for now
recharge
while i'm down
so i can get back up

i don't want to look back
at all those dark parts
i can't stop though
how can i
when they linger
under me
await
to attack
when they do
i'm brought back
i must restart

up

confusing
hurting
losing
separated
i went down
then up
so up that
the up stayed long and then
down became less strong
one day
the down had a lot more
when it did
i realized
the up is what i strive for
we can go down
up
down
up
through time
when down
you'll find your up
for i'm living proof there's less of it
the up and the down

i sit alone
almost every night
beneath my laptop light
hoping to write
something worth the fight
all for you
all for me
memories
shadows
pieces
tears
these feelings
all dance around me
flowing with ink
i let it all sink
within these pages
for you to keep for the ages
for me to see a dream

there is room to be rid of behaviours
there is room for new behaviours
there is room to improve my image
there is room to love my image
there is room to push myself
there is room to calm myself
there is room to pass the generations of trauma
there is room to remember the trauma
there is room out there
room for us all
room to simply be

that happiness
a glimpse of it
sprouting from sadness
eventually will
leak
seep
deep
protect
forever
be in me
as a reminder
when the pain hinders

i won't surrender to
depression
anxiety
trauma
harm
abuse
yet when it's so vile
within the stream
of these dark thoughts
i lay my armour down
and float away
but halfway to the darkest parts
i'll realize they are just thoughts
and i'll swim back up that stream
towards my paradise
i won't surrender
to the unwanted thoughts

the pain was creeping
now it's here
over there
i couldn't stop
it made me feel
and that's okay
let it in
then let it peal

i feel alone
i feel empty
i feel loveless
i feel angry
i feel sore
i feel used
i feel bad
i feel guilty
i feel ashamed
i feel abused
i feel all
that's just a part of living here
so every day
open your eyes
get up
see that morning dew
be sure to make it
towards that next day
don't ever be afraid
for the ones who love
will stay with you
so please you must
love you
even in all
the unexpected
love you
love you
love you
feel

we're getting older
missing young versions
losing old skin
saying goodbye
to real life angels
our kin
living hurts

they ask
are you a boy
or a girl
does it matter i say
in my mind
you uneducated fool
who raised you
probably another fool
go back to school

stopped
at a red light
with just yourself
no direction
in the worst case
reach out
so someone can aid you
with protection
on the way
to yourself
remember this
it's okay
to ask for help
for protection

the voices
the stares
scatter through the hall
stayed home from school
over 30 days away
pleading to die
hoping to get away
waiting on some help
from the unknown
i didn't know they knew me
even saw me
if they didn't come
i wouldn't be here
so thank you
to all the ones
who turned the voices down
i'm still here because of you

it was winning
i was losing
the good place didn't exist
i didn't want too either
yet somehow
i made it to the other side
i went through the turmoil
i am enough
i am alive
i am here now
i'm losing sometimes
we can't always win
but we can cross the finish line
as progress is a win

the patriarchy
take and take
stare and stare
break and break
yell and yell
hurt and hurt
through all that suffering
we band together
what are we worth
more than them
should we tell em
nah
they never listen

this life
it's all a game
unknown to us
yet we keep going
we must
to see the game finish
to find the gold trophy
to hold all the glory
and cherish it
when days become lonely

i love little things
that spark joy
could be video games
old memories soaked
in melted ice cream
or in the park
with a favourite toy
oh the little things
couldn't you stay

the children
have all the flavours
don't hide them
open them
let them see
and be seen

accelerate your
diverse self
hold it tight
do yourself right

a simple touch
i wanted
you wanted
then we left it at that

i was sad today
but happy too

some days
i wonder
where to go from here
but i think of you
him
them
all of us
i breathe in
i breathe out
i keep moving
so we can see
all of us
all of them
all together

all things
within intimacy
the touching
the holding
the kissing
the temperature
shared as a whole
you're allowed
to feel pleasure
we are humans
after all
so let it unfold
learn to love it
whenever you can

get to know yourself
be honest
look at them
stare in the mirror
finally realize you
honesty opens up doors

i'm a little late
to the party
but i'd rather
be late
than not live it

so what
it's just sex
it's inside us
we want it
it's human nature
it's love
it's fun
it's a game
you want it to
if not
that's okay
learn
take time
find your way

don't feel pressured
i wish i had a book
to help me feel
less inferior
it's something they didn't teach
way back when i wish
now they preach
thank god for that
for some it's too late
but thank you for us now
it numbs the hate

as a reminder
right now
this is your time
and it does not belong
to anyone else
just go about your day
and be yourself

the kiss
the undress
the hearts
both racing
you feel eyed
enjoyed by someone
hardly known
let it in
be one
enjoy the taste of sex

on the topic of sex…
i love it
with a stranger
falling deep within
slow motions of love
but not a forever love
a love for an hour or more
the senses touch my core
i love it
inside my body and outside
let me fall all over you
and you on me

the bed keeps me safe
i just want my space

touch it
love it
move it
now look at it
that body
all there is
hair or bare
only yours
to forever wear
so make room for care

breathe in
breathe out
go out
stay in
go to the dance or don't go
don't change for them
let joy come in
your way
in your own time
take chances
and when you can
don't forget all you are
open your door
when you can
go in

i'm still painting myself
it's a large canvas
i need to learn
all the colours
around me

keep doing the work
the perseverance
if you do
you may get there

i grew up with self loathing
always doubting
hurting
cutting
never breaking away from the pain
it always came
stronger than the heart
yet as older days came
the loathing dispersed
slowly
like a hard rain departing
i became parts of me
with me
finally
and i'm still going
thankfully

sometimes you must focus
on only you
and that's such
an attractive feeling

oh sex
it's the first touch
the meeting
the looking
the fun times
so hot
cute
funny
oh dear
what could go wrong…
love
experience
let it take you places

love the skin
from you kin
never ever
let them rip
dim
hurt
they will see
with all their marks
blood is the same
be what you are
inside and out

don't forget
to pleasure yourself
in mind
in body

who gave you the ultimate decision
to not educate the child
pressed and hidden
a whole cultured discarded
aren't children smart
it's what you all say
please teach them

hide in that walled garden
never doubt it
keep it safe
keep it hidden
until your ready
to water what shall sprout
then come on out

deep breaths first
do not let the fear control you
it will for a moment
i promise
you will get yourself out
please
i beg of you
the life you have
is so right
well and full
so stay strong

- you

we must have fun
let's go find it
together
alone
go

take a day
look at what you wear
don't ever let a stare
make you feel bare
take you
make it rare

don't be afraid to say goodbye
for whatever made you feel this way
must have brought such joy
there are always new beginnings
in life
in death
in goodbyes
at all times
they come and go
take note of the good
you'll be fine
and you'll know
when it's time

it takes time to build your own foundation
even more time securing it
if you do that
you'll be on your way
so take your time
in seeing
what builds
that foundation
it's one step at a time

thank you for playing
on my bed
with me
in me
the kisses
between the sheets
oh the heat
that never seeped
i love my bed
you within
all the sweats
all the games you played
we laid
on and on
until we both moved on
away from the same bed
thank you

sad days come
they linger
they stay
longer than joy
happy days
they take time
trust in that time
for those good days
are on the way

for people like us
most days we must thrust
through that hefty storm
eventually we find the calmest part
once found
we come out
let the call chase
bring forth your trust
through all shades
you can do it

in life
in love
in death
in hurting
in pain
we at times must perish the old self
to make room for the new
to be true
to be on the right way
we must make sure to cherish the new self

across the night
i meet you
kissing and touching
it's a delight
we have the privilege to share us
together alone
only the sheets know our secrets
that'll be it
once we part ways
but thank you
for those nights
that turned into days

in one fleeting moment
i finally love who i see
in that mirror
it took awhile
i want to hold them forever

the first 30 years
we only had control
for a short 12 years
the next 30 years
are all on us
live
do it
say yes
but i won't lie
i'm scared to
who isn't
let's all do it

annoyance
anger
impatience
they may come
remember positivity
for it makes way
for better days
so tomorrow
remember this

be good
you may receive good

making breakfast
having some tea
or even cleaning
i just try to breathe
here and there
when i am able
these things help
oddly enough

these feelings
these touches
how to describe them
impossible
to you they aren't real
to me
they're everything
i hide them
so i don't lose
you
what a fool
but a good fool
thank you
to the fool
who loved me
for a little while

make sure to focus
breathe
stay with now
for it will lead you
to the next day
breathe in
breathe out
5
4
3
2
1
breathe in
breathe out
it'll all be all right
get going okay
let's take this day

the most important relationship
is the one with yourself
know yourself worth
love it
cherish it
confide in it
be whole
don't hide it
it's all you
pure like new seeds planted
watch the important parts grow
love the time with yourself
in bed
on the road
during the messy parts
all the growths
all the decays
feel the most
of you
you can

just like that
we're meant to be together
all of the good in between
and everything messy
until it's time
that we're meant to be apart
that's okay
because what we had was art
now hanging in our louvre
that's in our heart

i have the power
the femininity
the masculinity
i can be whomever i wanna be
in all my colourful personas
in all my places
within me

the world is in a dark place
you are not alone
there are over 8 billion of us
most of us are on the good side…
we hope
that's all we can do
you must in the patches of the dark
find the little bits of spark
the random things
that make life seem lighter
find the sounds of laughter
the cat videos if you will
the random acts of kindness
even the beauty in the night
such as just sitting in the dark
watching the shooting stars
with your mother
it's these little bits of light
you can find
in hopes to drown out the nightmare
we need to find these places
to patch up the bad spaces
don't let go
we need you

i can't hold on to you forever
i'll be okay
once i am
i can feel the sun again
i'll be here
in the now
present
with all of me
leaving you to wonder
why it took so long
you'll want to come back
i won't let you
because i'll find a solitude
free of you
i'll be okay
then you'll be okay

your dream takes work
make note of that
let's get to it

do your happiness
let it fill you
to that feeling
of cakes
ice cream
ocean airs
first snows
child wows
let it be yours only
for these happy moments
are precious
so hold tight
to what you feel is right

that laugh
the foolish look
never change
it's what made me keep you
i love you
yet i'll never tell you
i never loved me
so please
continue
make me laugh
so i can feel okay
with you
with me

you're a whole person
with a whole heart
a whole view
a whole person with the world
at their fingertips
take your whole self
see the world
learn from it
be with it
let the world keep you whole
the good parts and bad parts
it's all you
you are a whole person
just like someone beside you

i'm grabbing all the happiness
all that i can see
keeping it so close
please don't leave me
i'm grasping all i can
in order to stay afloat

when
it's always on my mind
when will i love
when will i feel
when will i be freed from pain
when does the love come
haven't i been through enough
why hurt me
why hold me
why choke me
when will i ever be able to walk free
when will the eyes stop staring me down
when will i live calmly
when will i stop overthinking
when will i become one with me
when i'm 60
when i'm 70
when will i die
i always think of when
i hardly ever think of now
that's the problem
now is happening
we need to remember it
to see it
to hold it
not always think of when
so while we pass by
remember now
let now happen
so we remember when
that now was

remember
it is only one bad thought
it may bring many more
but they will go away
hope
thrive
grow
please continue
we need you here

today is just today
tomorrow is new

you say "what now?"
first you must rest
recharge
for you will get the best
within your time
trust the process
it'll let you grow
high above
to climb
so don't forget your time
hold all you've done close
soon you'll be on your way
and all that time
will be worth it

your shape comes and goes
your views on me still hurt
the suffering
the wronging
the abusing
the sins i've committed
due to the pain
are not written in stone
but you
as the strangler
you make up lie after lie
bring hurt after hurt
your opinions without an understanding
they are written in stone
enough of you
as to why i live like this
it's simple
this is me
after years of pain
gradually i won me back
to be the true me
because all your wrongs are wrong
outdated
broken
so on this journey of discovery
i'll keep finding me
the views
won't hurt so much
but you'll hurt
in a silent guilt
if ever you do find that understanding
come find me
apologize

you start the running
yet you're late
playing catch up
working on you
deeply starving and trying
for that validating form
still you're late
after all the crying
all the self hate
not gay enough
not black enough
not cultured enough
not this
not that
shut out
judged
cast aside
scared now
you'll never be ready
for that culture
all its sides
well remember
it takes time to realize
the outsides and ins
so keep running

29 – love, help, shelter, growing, now

my whole life
i've let people walk all over me
the guessing of my sexuality
the teasing of my stance
the looks
the yells
the slurs
i'm more than what you perceive
i know that now
so when i walk
i try to put that head high
see only me
the whole me
i walk from here to there
slaying the streets without a care
to filth with all who stare

time…
mysterious
scary
wonderful
wide eyed
dark
bright
all its horror and power
it's a part of us
locked in
to become
the hurting
the healing
on and on
we feel it all
the memories
the freshness
we're locked in
time keeps on reeling
until it's time to depart
so hold tight
and buckle up
for all the rides
during the times

all the cracks around us
all those shatters
they come forth
we can't stop it
we just keep going
because this life
it's a privilege
so feel that pain
let all be real
for its encounters
seduce
one by one
get by
so you can finally feel
all that's ahead of you

the version i am in right now
please stay
i must be with them
stay focused
i'll be strong today
and the next day
a promise to me
let tomorrow come
when it does
continue
with this soulful journey
of every version
that lay within
ready to begin

- evolve

you pinned me down
in my safe space
sucked the happiness away
made me cry
left a mark of shame
the mark may be gone now
but since the stamp
i've been triggered
all the trauma lingers
i know though
from the love around me
the happier i'll be
more so than when you marked me

in pain
in trauma
in abuse
we want goodbyes
please don't ever
let them take over
remember what they said
the love is there
so don't die
you'd dose you
in sour
instead make sure
to cry
let the pain run dry
don't worry
in time
it'll be gone
you'll keep the love
all for you
and move on
you'll be okay
i promise

feel that summer air
watch the sun sprinkle down warmth
let the views breathe in
watch the grass stained pants run
make sure your ice cream doesn't melt
enjoy that person with you now
for another day like this might not breathe
enjoy the laughter
the sounds of birds and lawnmowers
bring that smile people love
you aren't alone
if you want to be that's fine
let the days of unexpected joy
sink deep into the memories you need
during days of unrequested droughts
hold the memories
to feel

you may have been
a short time
in my life
but through it all
you made me tall
made it worthwhile
the hand holding
little kisses
camera clicks
all that came
i'm glad
it was a good video game
a good level
designed to make us fall
also to stand tall
alone
away from that short time
so thank you
for once being mine

i prefer the latter half
of the twenties
i see more
my first half
was learning
that's what it's all about
training for the thirties
i guess so…
could be
who knows

the sparkles on the water
from the suns smiling reflection
let that be your happiness
let the sparkles be your protection
in those places of emptiness
from ones who've brought the drought
let yourself twinkle right
don't bring their doubt

what goes up
must come down
when down
rise up
if not
fall if you must
but know
you've fallen before
and you'll make sure
to get back up
you can
and you will
i did

it grows you
it builds you
it helps you
it protects you
you're lucky if it did
fortunate it was there
for its one place
a lot of us don't fare
make sure to cherish
hold it
remember it
it was there to keep you warm
remember the home
the home you were born

there is a light
worth waiting for
keep pushing
open every door
close a few
turn around
until you find you

depression
it's time to let you go
you'll not take me
you almost did
i ruined your win
thank goodness
because i need it
it only took time
to find you don't belong
it's been a long time coming
to new beginnings
so thank you
goodbye

wait wait
stop stop
let me come back
one more hug
for one
just isn't enough
thank you
for letting me grow
because of you
i've been able to
so again
wait wait
stop stop
one more hug
again and again
for dad and mom
let me move on
forward
upward
i love you

thank you
nowhere to go
but up
up
and up

acknowledgments

These words found their way to me mostly in my 20s, especially in the latter half. Overflowing with so many unexplainable sensations. I was severely depressed, alone, happy, confused, excited. Severed straight down the middle. Two sides made of up and down. With the love unavailable around me. This book just wouldn't be possible. Even all of me.

Thank you to the ones who heard it first, listened to me, put up with me, loved me, spoiled me, and never stopped believing in me. You know who you are. The pages would be overwhelming with all the names. But a few do stand out.

To my rock, the fighter, the one and only Brittany. You've made me come into a better light all because of who you are as an individual. The smallest and biggest things. Thanks for being true to you and making us all laugh.

Rachel. My confidant, the one who understood this book first. You're someone who's been there through the thick and thin, all the childhood days. You're the brightest out of us all.

To Mrs. Z. and Mrs. M. Thank you for saving me from the bullies. And letting me hide away in the computer room during lunch.

Josh, thank you. You've always loved me and never cared who I was or how I acted as a kid. Thanks for letting me be the princess in our childhood filled imagination.

To my beautiful loving sisters, Alina, and Arden. I love writing, but words can't express enough how much you mean to me. Both of you are always there for me with a phone call or wild text or answering the phone at 3am in the morning when I'm running from the clubs. I love you both. Thanks for being my sisters. Thanks for the childhood.

And to all the animals I have/had, thanks for laying with me, listening to me cry and all the kisses.

To the greatest people in the whole wide universe, my mother and father. You have supported me to places I thought impossible. My mom and dad are who mothers and fathers should be. Thanks for spoiling me, being my biggest supporters and always pushing me even when I didn't want to push myself anymore. I love you for evermore. All of you.

And thanks to you, the reader, the one who has invaded my mind, the good and the bad, and understood it all. Here's for more places to be within. So, stay tuned.

Thanks to me. To you. For being alive.

Xoxo

Manufactured by Amazon.ca
Acheson, AB